To My Rainbow Baby with Love

This book is dedicated with love to:

_____

To My Rainbow Baby with Love

Written by Tamekia McCauley
Illustrated by Serineh Eliasian
Copyright © 2015

This book is dedicated to my rainbow baby Rocki and to the families who have experienced this difficult circumstance. I hope this book helps you find comfort today and forever. To my mommy friends from "BC" thank you for your friendship and support through our shared heartache and triumphs. ~TM

You wondered about the baby in the picture frame and I knew it was time.

For me to tell you about another child I called mine.

I have a story about a member of our family you never knew.

Mommy and daddy struggled to find the right words that we would use to tell you.

We had a baby before you who did not get to come home with mommy and daddy.

Sometimes babies are sick and don't live long sadly.

Mommy and daddy were very heartbroken.

For a long time we bottled up our feelings and left them unspoken.

People sent us beautiful flowers and nice letters.

We appreciated all of the kindness; it made us feel better.

Time passed and the doctor told us we were having a rainbow baby.

Mommy and daddy were excited from the start.

During our sadness you helped heal our hearts.

I know this is difficult to hear and it is okay to feel sad.

These are normal feelings when someone we love has passed.

When we lose someone we love they always stay near and dear.

As a family we will do something special to remember our loved one year after year.

Rainbows lift our spirits and appear across the sky after the rain.

You don't realize it, but for mommy and daddy you did the same.

Most days are now spent with laughter and grins.

Yet some nights we sit thinking quietly about what could have been.

Please always remember you are not a replacement for your sibling.

You'll be your own person: happy, kind, and super amazing.

We're so grateful for you, our perfect rainbow.

About the Author: Tamekia McCauley is a mom and educator with a doctorate from Baker University. She enjoys spending time with her family and traveling. Her daughter Genevieve was diagnosed with Trisomy 18, a rare chromosomal condition. This book was written in her memory.

About the Illustrator: Serineh Eliasian is an illustrator with a degree in graphic design from the University of Art in Tehran, Armenia. Illustrating children's books is her passion.

Resources:

Still Standing Magazine

www.stillstandingmag.com

Pregnancy after Loss Support

www.pregnancyafterlosssupport.com

Support Organization for Trisomy 18, 13, and Other Related Disorders

www.trisomy.org

Project Heal

www.carlymarieprojectheal.com

Subsequent Pregnancy after Loss Support

www.spals.com

Official site of Pregnancy and Infant Loss Day

www.October15.com